A BOY AND A JAGUAR

WRITTEN BY
Alan Rabinowitz

ILLUSTRATED BY
Cátia Chien

HOUGHTON MIFFLIN HARCOURT

Boston New York

To all those who have found their voice,

and who use it to speak for others in need.

—A.R.

For the many teachers in my life who helped me find my voice.

—C.C.

Text copyright © 2014 by Alan Rabinowitz

Illustrations copyright © 2014 by Catia Chien

www.hmhbooks.com

The text of this book is set in Chaparral Pro.

The illustrations are acrylic and charcoal pencil.

Library of Congress Cataloging-in-Publication Data

Rabinowitz, Alan, 1953–

A boy and a jaguar / written by Alan Rabinowitz ; illustrated by Catia Chien.

pp. cm

ISBN 978-0-547-87507-1

1. Rabinowitz, Alan, 1953—Juvenile literature. 2. Wildlife conservationists—United States—Biography—Juvenile literature.
3. Panthera—Conservation—Juvenile literature. I. Chien, Catia, illustrator. II. Title.

QL83.R33 2013

333.95'975092—dc23

[B]

2012025531

Manufactured in China

SCP 10 9 8 7 6 5 4 3 2 1

4500455685

I'm standing in the great cat house at the Bronx Zoo. *Why is this jaguar kept in a bare room?* I wonder.

I lean toward my favorite animal and whisper to her.

"What are you doing?" my father asks.

I try to explain, but my mouth freezes, just as I knew
it would. I am a stutterer. If I try to push words out,
my head and body shake uncontrollably.

The teachers at school put me in a class for disturbed children.

"He's not disturbed," my parents say.

"We're sorry," the teachers answer, "but whenever he tries to speak, he disrupts the class."

The teachers think I am broken. Am I?

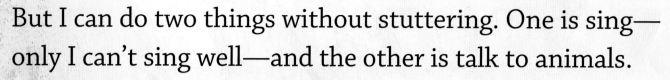

But I can do two things without stuttering. One is sing—
only I can't sing well—and the other is talk to animals.

Every day I come home from class and go straight
to the closet in my room. I bring out my pets—
a hamster, a gerbil, a green turtle, a chameleon,
and a garter snake. I close the door and talk to them.

Without stuttering.

I tell them my dreams. I tell them that I
want to be able to speak like everyone else.

I know that my pets listen and understand. Animals can't get the words out, just as I can't get the words out. So people ignore or misunderstand or hurt them, the same way people ignore or misunderstand or hurt me.

I make a promise to my pets.

I promise that if I can ever find my voice, I will be *their* voice and keep them from harm.

My parents try everything to help me: doctor after
doctor, medicine, and hypnosis. Nothing works.

But my father knows the one thing that *does* work. He takes me to the great cat house at the Bronx Zoo. I go straight to the cage with the lone jaguar, lean over the railing, and put my face against the bars.

I whisper my promise to her. Fluently.

I get through school by learning tricks that
stutterers learn. I learn when not to speak,
when to avoid situations, and when to just
not be around people.

When I'm in college, my parents enroll me in an experimental program. There, I'm told that I am a stutterer and will always be a stutterer. Always. But the teacher tells me that if I work hard, I can be a completely fluent stutterer. I think about how my mouth moves and air flow, and for the first time in years, I can speak without stuttering.

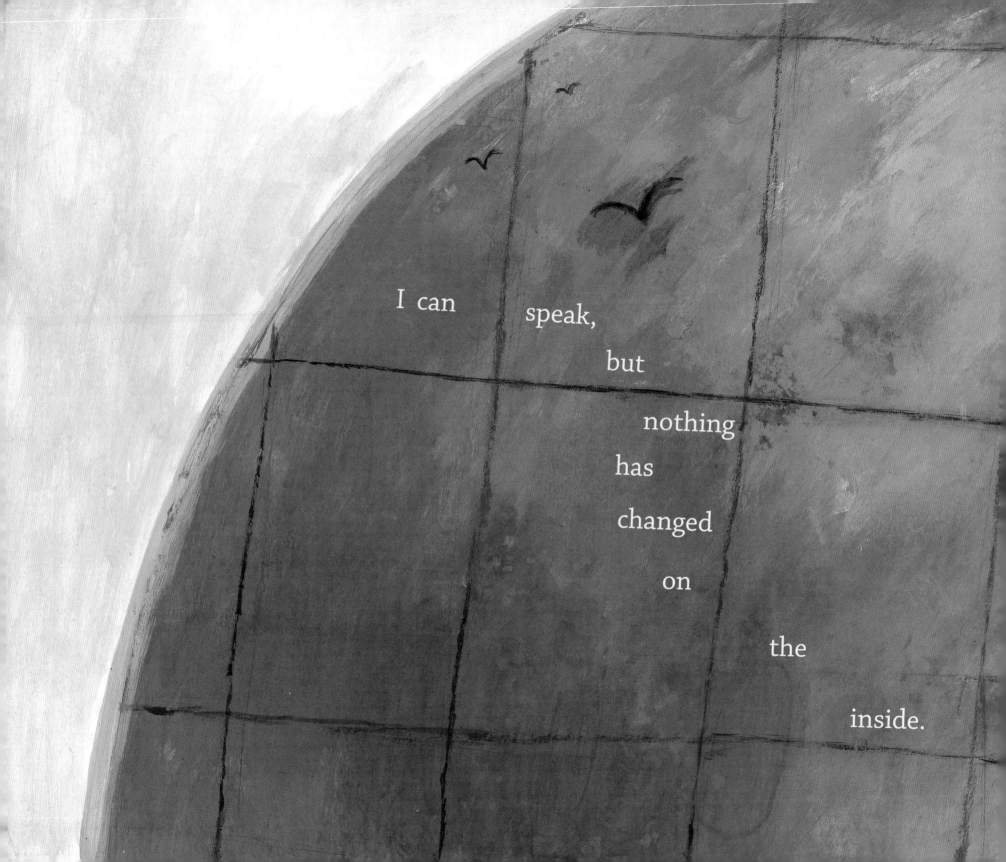

I can speak, but nothing has changed on the inside.

I go to the Great Smoky Mountains to study black bears.

Alone in the forest with the animals, I am at home.

Later, in Belize, I am the first person to study jaguars.

The jungle makes me feel more alive than I have ever felt.

I learn how to follow and capture jaguars for study before releasing them back into the wild. I am happy!

But as fast as I catch jaguars and gather information to help them, hunters are killing them. They fear the animals and prize their bodies as trophies.

I need to get more areas protected for the jaguars. I want to keep the promise I made to the pets in my closet. I have a voice now to speak for animals.

In the capital city of Belize, in the office of the prime minister, I am given fifteen minutes to make my case.

Fifteen minutes.

I can't stutter and distract from my message.
I have to convince one of the poorest countries
in Central America, with no protected areas in
the entire country, that it has to save jaguars.

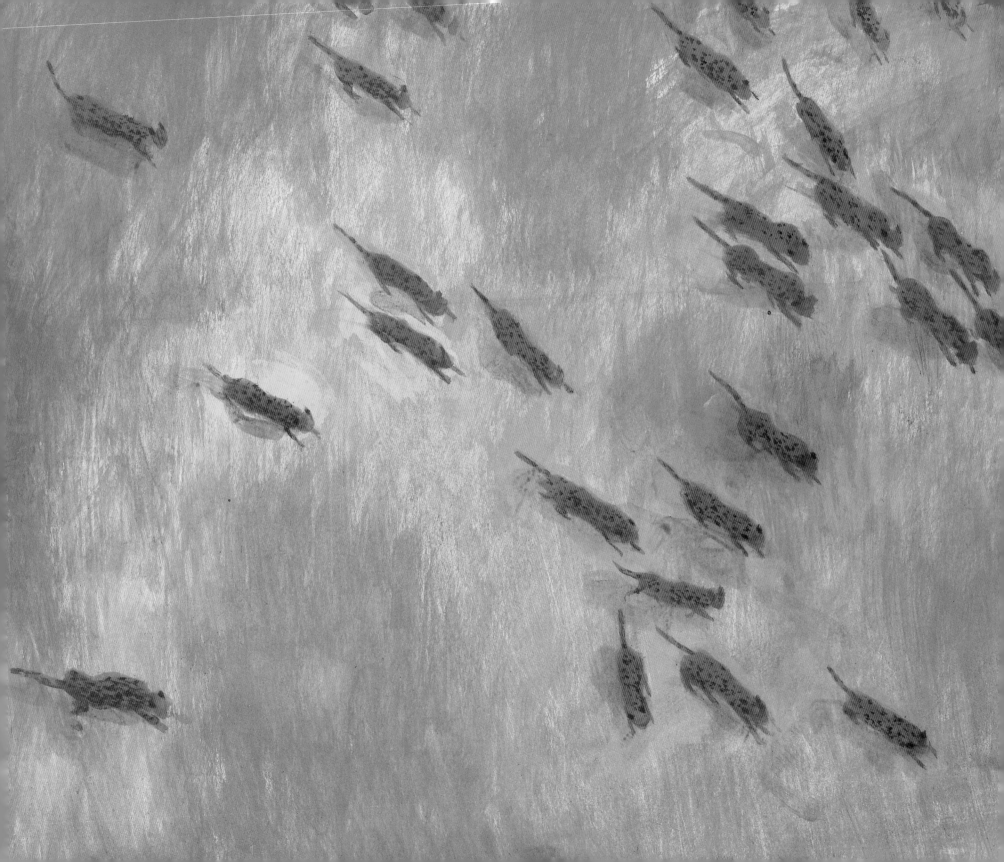

Later that day, the prime minister votes to set up the world's first and only jaguar preserve.

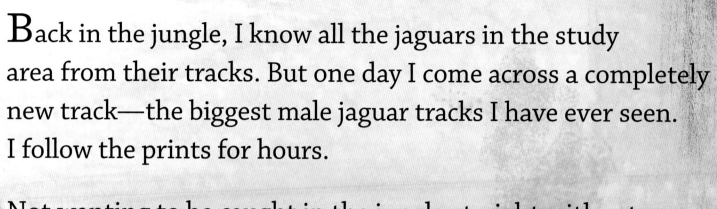

Back in the jungle, I know all the jaguars in the study area from their tracks. But one day I come across a completely new track—the biggest male jaguar tracks I have ever seen. I follow the prints for hours.

Not wanting to be caught in the jungle at night without a flashlight, I turn around to go back to camp.

There, right behind me, is the jaguar.

He must have been following *me!*

I know I should feel frightened, but I squat down and look into the jaguar's eyes, just as I had with the sad old female at the Bronx Zoo. But this animal isn't sad. In this animal's eyes are strength and power and sureness of purpose.

We are both whole.

We are both at home.

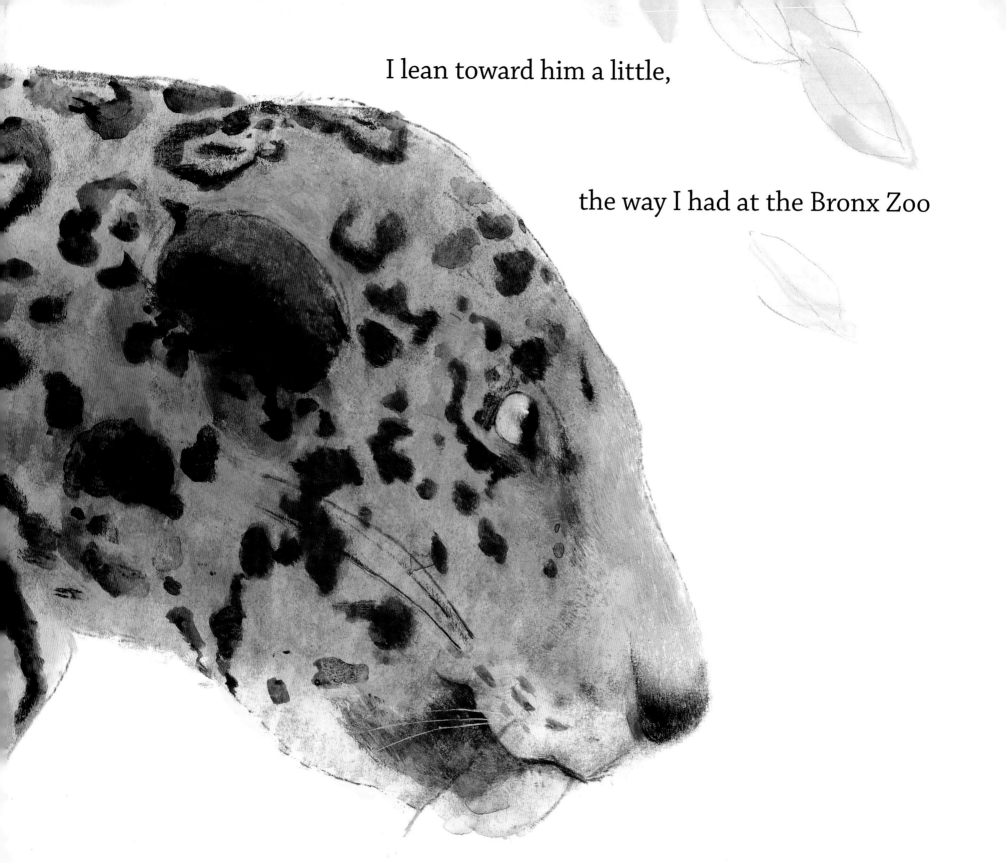

I lean toward him a little,

the way I had at the Bronx Zoo

so many years before.

"Thank you," I whisper.